The Psy...........

Manufactured in the United States of America

Dedication

To my daughter Ayanna. I love you!

About the Author

Bakari has been practicing no-gi Brazilian Jiu-jitsu since 2004 and BJJ with a gi since 2008. He has a Purple Belt in BJJ and a Green Belt in Judo. Akil also has written about grappling for *Black Belt Magazine* and his blog, *Jiujitsu365*, has been nominated twice for "Best BJJ Blog" by the *Fightworks Podcast*.

Akil holds a Ph.D. in Mass Communication from Florida State University. He is currently a Professor and has taught and counseled thousands of people over the years in areas related to graduate education, mass media and how to be more effective communicators.

Other Grappling books by Bakari Akil:

20 Ways to Improve Grappling Skills off the Mats

Grappling 101: How to Avoid getting Bullied on the Mat

Tapmonster: Ideas on Grappling for BJJ and Submission Grapplers

Grappling for Newbies: What every BJJ and Submission Grappler should know!

The Lazy Man's Guide to Grappling

Grappling Games

Do Most Fights go to the Ground?

Table of Contents

Foreword

Grappling is a smash-mouth activity. It is a put your beer down and let's settle this type of martial art. Man vs. man, woman vs. man, child vs. man, it is one of the ultimate 'prove it' combat sports. Yet, once you get past the rough and challenging aspect of submission wrestling it's easy to see that grappling is much more than that. It is also a very cerebral activity.

For the uninitiated, the level of analysis, forethought and planning that grapplers put into the combat sport can be astounding. As soon as grapplers get bitten by that 'bug,' class is no longer sufficient enough to quell the curiosity of the budding grappler. Questions on positioning, angles, entries, blocks, defenses and how to become more dominant causes the grappler to seek out and pore over instructionals (books, videos and DvDs), read blogs and listen to podcasts that dissect grappling into minutiae that upsets any non-grappler within earshot.

As a grappler who has been involved with the sport for more than a decade I am also guilty of exploring submission wrestling from every possible angle. It is difficult not to see a connection to grappling in everything I say, hear or do. I am also an academic, so by default, I apply academic theory and research to my grappling experiences. Thus, *Psychology of Brazilian Jiu-jitsu* (BJJ) was born.

Psychology is the study of mental processes and behaviors. By studying our psyches, we hope to learn how to successfully navigate our world and become more capable in our endeavors. As the goal of theory is explanatory and predictive power, using psychology theories can help us to understand some of the existential questions behind our art and can help us to create better models for training and success. In other instances, it is just plain fun to think about.

The application of psychology and research to submission wrestling is relatively new and in many cases non-existent, so this book is more of an exploration of what is possible. It covers a broad range of topics and doesn't hesitate to introduce counterintuitive thought for the reader to ponder and digest.

Will you agree with everything that is written in this book?

—

Probably not.

However, what I have attempted to do in this book is to whet your appetite to see how psychological and communication theory can be applied specifically to grappling and not just in a generic sports psychology sense.

Through the use of short small essays, *Psychology of BJJ* talks about what it's like to be the new guy, problems with warm-ups, success by default, immersive environments, why you can't always be nice in practice and even asks outright, "Are you happy?"

If that is not enough, it also discusses why you absolutely must not avoid better grapplers, tells you what type of grappler you are and why your team is just as important as your coach. Additionally, *Psychology of BJJ* delves into the unconscious mind and talks about easy ways to improve by taking simple steps you probably never thought about before. It also discusses quirky, but valid, psychological theory, based on new research that can make a difference in your game.

I hope you enjoy it!

Bakari Akil II, PhD

a.k.a. JiuJitsu365

New Guy: Territory and Dominance

Six months after I started BJJ a guy came to our school and said he was thinking about taking Jiu-jitsu. My instructor, David, paired us up and through small pieces of conversation I learned that he was a former high school wrestler. He also let me know that he was not just any former high school wrestler; he was a state champion for his division. That's fine; I like it when people tell me the truth about their experience. However, I also got the distinct feeling that he was letting me know that he wasn't going to be an easy mark and most likely, I was going to be manhandled by him. We had started the dance.

When it was time to spar I could see that he had every intention of showing he was the alpha-male as there was no give and take with his grappling. I could feel that he wanted to 'win' at any cost. I had a year of Judo experience so I was able to withstand his initial single and double leg attempts and eventually tripped him to the ground. He turned onto his hands and knees to get up and I jumped on his back, sunk in my hooks (feet around his waist) and applied the rear naked choke (RNC). After we slapped hands again, we went through the exact same sequence. I tapped him, both times, with a RNC. After the second time, though, he slammed his fist into the mat after I let him go.

He never came back to our academy after that day.

Do I know the exact reason why he chose not to return? No. Yet, I have a good idea. This scenario has been played out, countless times, in every grappling club in the world. New people come into the club and they have to negotiate their entry. Some can accept that there is a pecking order and they may have to start at the bottom. For others, it is too much of a shock and they balk at the thought of starting over from scratch. The wrestler I faced was dripping with confidence. If confidence were sold in a box, it would have had his face on it. I don't think he expected to lose to one of the lowest ranking members in the gym. He probably expected to dominate most of us and take his place alongside our instructor at the end of the day. As a recent newcomer, however, I wasn't in the mood to let that happen, so the unspoken battle began. This jockeying for position is rarely talked about in grappling circles, but just because it is not said out loud doesn't mean it isn't real.

As the child of a military man, we were always on the move. Every two years from the ages of 5 to 18, I moved with my family from one military base to the next. We moved so much that after a while I stopped saying goodbye to my friends before I would leave. I would just 'disappear.'

My adult life hasn't been much different, as I have transferred quite a few times for jobs. At the college where I am currently employed I have only worked there for two years. All this constant movement means that when I move for jobs, I also change grappling schools.

Thus, I am quite familiar with the role of the new guy. As a child this always meant new friendships and sometimes exciting new environments. It also meant new bullies and as a teenage male always having to prove myself to different sets of testosterone filled adolescents.

As an adult being the new guy takes on a different meaning. The craziness of schoolyard bullying goes away and is often replaced by passive aggressive workplace behavior from colleagues and the occasional office tyrant. In grappling schools, it is a little less serious in my experience, but it still exists.

Many of you may already know what I'm talking about, but there are a few who may have been lucky enough to have no 'new guy' experiences in grappling. You may have trained at the same school since it opened its doors. That's fine. It just means that you are on the other side of the coin. But all of us participate. No matter where you are in the equation and regardless of the severity or pleasantness of the 'new guy' experience, the back and forth dance must take place.

Robert Sommers in his book _Personal Space: The Basis of Behavioral Design_ (2008), talks about two things that affect people's behavior when first meeting each other. Those things are "territoriality" and "dominance." Sommers asserts that most people avoid trouble because they are fully aware of areas that are 'safe' territories (usually their own) and avoid those that aren't. Further, because they are intimately familiar with the power hierarchies that exist between them and other people within their own environment there is usually no need for conflict (dominance) because arrangements, whether conscious or not, have already been determined. This explains why most academies are trouble free environments. Rivalries exist, but for the most part, they have already been negotiated on the mat.

Now imagine the 'new guy' entering the grappling school. The people within the gym already have their arrangements in place. They know their roles, who the senior students are, who can beat who, their general standing in the scheme of things and written and unwritten protocols of the organization. The new grappler, regardless of rank, upsets this balance and it has to be restored.

The established members of the group only have to deal with the new grappler once or twice when negotiating a relationship, regardless if the outcome is positive or negative. The new grappler has a lot more to do because he has to negotiate terms with everyone in the organization.

As Sommers expressed in his research, established members use territorial claims in negotiating with newcomers and let them know immediately where they stand. These types of claims are often verbal and serve as gentle warnings. For instance, in a work environment an established member may say, "Don't worry about these invoices, I always handle these." Usually, the new person (without rank) would respond to such statements with deference until he learns where his own boundaries begin and end.

However, if that fails then 'dominance' techniques will be used, depending of course, on the level of aggressiveness the established members are willing to display. But, since the BJJ community does not tolerate such hyper-aggressive behavior, newcomers are usually at the receiving end of passive aggressive activity. Examples of the treatment handed out to 'new guys' include being called a "newbie" or "rookie;" being told an inappropriate joke to see how they will respond; being ignored by someone even after being properly introduced; having to listen to rants such as "you young people are all over the place;" and being subjected to the "stick with me and I'll show you the ropes" conversations. In severe cases, established members try to assert themselves by yelling or using threats.

What can be done?

Well, one major way to lessen 'new guy' woes is to make sure you learn as much as you can about your new academy and the roles you will serve before you join. I often scour the web and check out a new club and its members before I step through the door. By analyzing everything I can find, I develop a good idea of what to expect. Additionally, asking what the instructor will expect of you and what type of environment you should anticipate is a good idea. You may be surprised by how much information you receive and the response in general.

Unwritten rules and informal codes always play a role in any organization and sometimes can only be learned on the mat, but knowing the rules, responsibilities and duties expected of you as a member of an academy can go a long way in avoiding hassles and 'stepping on toes.'

Is there a cure-all to avoid some of the pinch of being the new guy? Not really, because people can applaud, resent or be indifferent to your arrival for the same reasons. But knowing that friction can and will occur and that its most likely not you, but the circumstance, will help you deal with situations more calmly as they arise.

Do Warm-ups Hinder Progress? Or "I've got 7 seconds of fight in me" and I used it all in the warm-up.

I've got 7 seconds of fight in me. **- Kevin James, Comedian**

Psychologist, Carle Beuke, Ph.D., wrote an interesting article titled, *How to become an expert.* He talked about using deliberate practice to improve one's skills and abilities. For those who are unaware, deliberate practice is where you break down an activity into chunks and slowly work on that chunk until you master it. Then you move on to the next chain in the series.

What I found interesting about his article is that when he discusses sports, he specifically mentions the idea of excessive warm-ups, which is a frequently debated topic in BJJ and grappling circles. Beuke writes:

Deliberate practice requires pushing yourself to perform slightly better than you normally would. You need to be at your best to achieve this. This means being well-rested and fresh. For this reason, doing an hour of cardio to 'warm up' for sports practice is not helpful.

Before we go further, I must admit I am not in favor of grueling warm-ups. On the other hand, as time passes, age and weight affects my ability to accurately assess why I am not a fan of them. My lack of fondness for warm-ups has built up slowly over the years because there have been many times where I have been worn out before drilling started, or worse, injured. Often during these types of warm-ups my lower back muscles seize up into a pretzel, my abdominals lock up or I get calf cramps or a cramp that curls my foot into a little ball. After that, class is all about survival.

I can understand a brief, 10-minute warm-up where we jog a little, perform some grappling specific exercises such as shrimping, bridging, rolling, break-falls and then proceed to light stretching. But what has happened over the years is that Crossfit, P90x, Insanity and other hardcore training techniques such as Tabatha drills have seeped their way into the 'warm-up' and many classes often become an endurance challenge before you can gain BJJ knowledge.

I think this happens for a couple of reasons. The first is because I am dubious that most instructors aged 18 to 32 years old truly understand that once you hit a certain age the body does not just 'bounce back' after exercise. This may lead to a callousness or indifference to the plight of those who struggle because of a complete lack of awareness of what the older grappler is experiencing. Further, aches, pains and injuries accumulate over the years and are easy to aggravate. As a large segment of grapplers are 30 and above it would behoove instructors to be mindful of this.

Additionally, many younger grapplers have different expectations than older grapplers. Some want to open their own grappling school one day. Other young grapplers dream about being BJJ, Judo or Sambo champions. Then they want to parlay that experience into becoming an MMA champion. A good number of these guys can't figure out why everyone doesn't want to train as hard as they do and get frustrated by it.

To borrow from Seinfeld, when he was younger, becoming Batman or Superman wasn't a dream, *it was an option*. But for older grapplers, they want to make sure they don't get injured so they can have the **option** of going in to work the next day or so they can attend to their children's needs that night and the day after. This means that they have to avoid 'overdoing it' in class. Plus, older grapplers can't afford to live the austere life of a fighter because they usually have spouses, kids, mortgages and job responsibilities. Of course, experiences and desires vary but if you've been around the grappling scene for more than a month you understand what I am talking about.

I train at a school that is not competition oriented and I appreciate this, but a lot of people do not have this choice and train at schools that have a lot of students focused on MMA and that compete in grappling tournaments. It is my assertion that this often leads to warm-ups that are too rough.

As Beuke alluded to, when the body is excessively taxed it is very difficult to perform drills properly. If the individual doesn't quit during the session (and I have never seen anyone quit in 10 years of grappling) they will resort to going through the motions and will have difficulty focusing on the specifics. Further, they may not be able to drill with precision due to fatigue. This can lead to bad habits or injury during techniques that require attention to detail such as throws and takedowns.

As a submission wrestler I know that grappling is not meant to be easy. I also know that there is a fine line between pushing grapplers hard to achieve excellence and overworking them. My purpose in writing about this and raising questions is not to bash instructors, young people or grapplers who are easily able to cope with any warm-ups thrown their way. It is to remind people that warm-ups for grappling should be intended to prepare students for drills and sparring (rolling) that occurs afterward. It shouldn't drain them of their capacity to learn and leave them unable to get the most out of their training session.

Making Success Unconscious in Grappling

We slapped hands, as is customary before a grappling session. His demeanor was calm and he gave no indication when we were talking earlier that he was ultra-aggressive. We postured for a brief second, sizing each other up. Without warning he leapt into the air with both of his arms, legs and torso coming my way. Reflexively, I placed both hands in the middle of his chest and pushed him downward. There was a thunderous sound when he hit the mat. We both looked at each other for a moment; me startled by his aggression and he by my quick but explosive defense.

What happened that moment lies at the heart of what Malcolm Gladwell wrote about in his book, *Blink: the power of thinking without thinking*. I am by no means an expert at Brazilian Jiu-jitsu (BJJ). But I have been practicing BJJ as well as Judo for a combined 10 years. Each class we drill takedowns, takedown defense, how to hold someone down, how to protect yourself if taken down and how to make a person submit through a combination of chokes, joint locks and other nefarious techniques.

Once we finish drills we then 'roll' or wrestle with each other to solidify the techniques we practice. Where I train, new and advanced techniques are introduced often. Yet, they are extensions of basic techniques, so it is not uncommon to practice the basics hundreds of times. We practice to the point where carrying out a technique becomes an unconscious process. Or what Gladwell would describe as a Level 2 event. Level 1 is reserved for tasks where we must be actively engaged in order to get something done. Unfamiliar tasks and unknown variables cause us to perk up and pay attention in these situations.

At a speech at the University of Washington, Anthony Greenwald, Ph.D., who Gladwell also profiles in his book, discussed the unconscious manner in which we operate when performing certain tasks. He asserted that we are comfortable in these situations and can go through the motions without having to think about what to do next. He cited riding a bicycle, going through a checkout lane and driving as actions where we don't often give our full attention. In fact, he went a step further and said we spend most of our lives in Level 2.

As grapplers, we have to ask ourselves tough questions. For example: How many of the tasks related to becoming a success do you complete at Level 2? How many 'reps' have you done; how much 'film' have you watched; how many 'plays' have you devised and practiced and how many 'competitions' have you entered in order to make what you do an unconscious process?

Sure, we must be fully present when engaging in any activity. But as grapplers, the more we can focus on the big picture and not on the individual steps the better off we will be. The more techniques we are able to transfer to a Level 2 status, the faster our reaction times will be and we will be able to focus more on sequences and chains of techniques as opposed to thinking, "What do I do next?"

Immersion and Environment

Daniel Coyle, author of *The Talent Code*, went on a quest to find out why some people seem to develop massive levels of talent while others do not. His major thesis was that myelin (glial cells), which are fatty deposits that form protective sheaths around nerve fibers (axons) throughout your neuronal network, allow electrochemical impulses to travel much more quickly. The more layers of myelin that develop, the better. This build up is what allows expert grapplers to always be a split second faster than you.

He equated this build-up of myelin as the difference between possessing a broadband or dial-up Internet connection. What's even more significant about this is that impulses seem to jump from one myelin node to the next so they do not have to travel the entire distance that it would have to on a non-myelinated network. For people who achieve high levels of ability this build-up occurs through slow and fast deliberate practice of actions repeated thousands of times.

But that is just the 'science' behind his book. Anyone who has had a General Psychology, Anatomy and Physiology course or has read any books about the brain knows this information. To me, the most fascinating part of his book dealt with the people and more importantly the environments they developed their talents in.

One of the chapters dealt with how Brazil became a powerhouse in soccer. On a visit, Coyle describes what he observed when walking through one block in a city in Brazil. He counted 50 symbols, before he gave up, of how much the sport is revered. He saw boys walking down the street juggling soccer balls with their feet, people watching a soccer match in a pub and men playing a mini-form of soccer called futsal on what looked like a basketball court. The environment is geared toward the one thing that a soccer fan or player loves most and that is soccer.

Making it Personal

When it comes to grappling, how often do you find yourself in an immersive environment such as the one Coyle describes? Common folk wisdom such as "birds of a feather flock together" and "if you lay down with dogs you'll get fleas" is abundant and warns us about the negative consequences of associating with the wrong crowd or being in a 'bad' environment. Yet, how often do we remind ourselves that we should always be searching for the optimal environment to advance our own interests?

At times, as long as the environment isn't overtly 'hurting' our progress we may overlook the fact that it isn't **helping** to increase our development, nourish our talent or prod us to increase our capabilities. But this approach doesn't promote the growth and excellence that many of us are searching for if we find ourselves in non-optimal environs. If your quest for excellence has you puzzling on what to do next, maybe finding or developing an optimal grappling environment may be the spark you need.

Ask yourself these questions:

How immersive is your environment? Is it set up so that it encourages your growth and development in grappling? Do the people around you help promote your interest in the art? How can your environment become more immersive so that your skill increases naturally and even when you are not in practice?

Are you a Happy Grappler?

If you've ever been to a mall, you may have been involved in the following scenario. A person with a clipboard locks her eyes on you. She shouts out a pleasantry followed by a plea to fill out her 'survey' for marketing research. "It will take just a moment," she says as she moves in your direction. You look down, speed up and shift lanes. If you had a football, you'd probably score.

Mall marketers aside, questionnaires don't always have to be for the benefit of social, commercial or scientific endeavors. They can also benefit our grappling lives. Let me explain.

Sometimes we may have a feeling that our experience with grappling isn't quite what we would like it to be. However, we might not be able to pinpoint the source of our dissatisfaction. All we know is that our level of 'happiness' and enjoyment of the combat sport isn't quite right.

A good way to pinpoint this dissatisfaction so we can begin to effectively deal with it is to create a Life Ratings Scale.

Put simply, a Life Ratings Scale requires you to create a list of all areas in your life that you consider important to having a life of quality and enjoyment. Next using a Likert-type scale from 0 to 5, with 0 as extremely unsatisfied and 5 being very satisfied, you rate each of the categories.

By using this technique for grappling you can gain a very clear picture of where your areas of dissatisfaction lay. Then you can begin to come up with ways to address them.

A sample Life Ratings Scale for Submission Wrestling can be:

Academy 0 1 2 3 4 5

Instructor 0 1 2 3 4 5

Senior Students 0 1 2 3 4 5

Students of Same Rank 0 1 2 3 4 5

Atmosphere 0 1 2 3 4 5

Training 0 1 2 3 4 5

Time Classes are Available 0 1 2 3 4 5

Fees 0 1 2 3 4 5

Once you create your most important categories and rate them you can break them down further to isolate key areas you would like to target.

For instance, "Fees" can be broken down into:

Cost of Training 0 1 2 3 4 5

Seminar Costs 0 1 2 3 4 5

Gi Cost 0 1 2 3 4 5

BJJ Equipment 0 1 2 3 4 5

Media (DvDs, Books, etc.) 0 1 2 3 4 5

or

You can create a category called Fitness:

Weight 0 1 2 3 4 5

Strength 0 1 2 3 4 5

Diet 0 1 2 3 4 5

Anaerobic Endurance 0 1 2 3 4 5

Flexibility 0 1 2 3 4 5

Or it could be based on Techniques or Positions:

Takedowns 0 1 2 3 4 5

Guard 0 1 2 3 4 5

Side Control 0 1 2 3 4 5

Mount 0 1 2 3 4 5

Back Mount 0 1 2 3 4 5

Submissions 0 1 2 3 4 5

Defense 0 1 2 3 4 5

Escapes 0 1 2 3 4 5

This covers the basics but you can be as detailed as you wish. By clearly defining regions of dissatisfaction in your grappling experience and then isolating exactly what ails you, you can then create a program or make the changes necessary to improve your enjoyment of grappling. Periodic checks (every month, 3 months, 6 months or year) using the same techniques can let you see your progress.

I created this scale for my usage and it helps me to determine my level of satisfaction in many facets of my grappling journey. It is a wonderful tool to help you make any adjustments you feel necessary and I recommend it to all.

Why you have to wrestle against better grapplers

All-star defensive tackle and NFL Hall of Famer, Warren Sapp, in his book, *The Sapp Attack*," talks about his childhood and his struggle with playing with his older brothers. As the youngest (by six years) he watched each of them become star athletes in their own right and loved to hang out with them. But in order to do so he had to play sports with the big boys.

Sapp described his initiation into sports as brutal. He said he always prayed that he could win against his brothers and his friends, in any sport. He even prayed for the ability to 'just' score a point. However, his tries often ended in failure and frustration. Sapp said that these sessions ended with him going home and crying when he was in the safety of his room.

As a grappler, you can probably identify with Warren Sapp and your own struggle against experienced and better grapplers. It is not fun to get schooled every time you grapple on the mat. Whether as the new guy or because you're having a bad day or due to a slump, having to go against better grapplers is tough to do. It is even more difficult when the better grappler is someone you think you should beat.

If you are like most, you probably face the challenge and take the 'beating.' However, we all know that guy who will only wrestle the guys he can tap out, if given a choice. Further, if we examine our own inadequacies, we probably give ourselves a break every now and again. I can recall one open mat session, shortly after receiving my purple belt, where I received a 'drubbing' by two senior purple belts for an hour straight. The last five minutes of class I hopped at the chance to wrestle a Blue belt just so I could have a little dignity when I walked out of the building that day. As you can guess, most of us are guilty in taking the easy route to some extent.

Yet, when the easy way is the only route we take as grapplers, we get into trouble. If done on a consistent basis a grappler is shunning the potential benefits for immediate glory.

The plus side to Warren Sapp's adventures is that when he played against guys his own age and size he destroyed them. There was absolutely nothing they could do with him. The lessons he learned playing against the big boys helped him become a dominant player, which lasted through high school, his tenure as a Miami Hurricane and through 13 seasons in the NFL. By playing with the vets as a rookie, Sapp increased the pace of his learning curve.

Your learning curve increases as well when you grapple with better players. They expose gaps in your game, give advice to help shore up your deficiencies and they motivate you to work harder. You have to strike a delicate balance to make sure you don't become overly discouraged, but if done with care you can improve by leaps and bounds.

For instance, as a Blue belt, I attended an academy where I was a senior student. I regularly handed out beatings. Yet, I knew something was missing. When I switched schools where I was once again on the low end of the totem pole, I repeatedly got smashed. It took two months before I could regroup and begin to hold my own with all of the Purple, Brown and Black belts. I also saw my progression when other Blue Belts or new White belts would join the school. I handled Blue Belts like White Belts and gave Purple Belts more trouble than they were seeking.

If I had maintained my Blue Belt (senior student) path I would have been deluding myself and would have kept thinking I was better than I really was. It was important for me to train with guys much better than I and it is important for you too.

Process or Results Oriented Approach to Jiu-jitsu

In communication and psychology, the terms Results Oriented and Process Oriented are used to describe people's approach to communicating with others, tackling tasks and competing. Although neither approach is inherently good or bad, it is best to know which approach is more useful when training in sports.

Before discussing how the Process or Results Oriented approaches relate to grappling, think about what type of grappler you are. Remember, there is no right or wrong here; you will just be assessing your approach.

When you consider your overall grappling mindset, are you more concerned with progress or winning? Are you concerned about being the best you can be or being the best? In practice do you work on parts of your game you consider weak or do you only rely on your strongest techniques against your rolling partners? When you compete, does a loss cause to you to descend into a funk or do you recognize the good points of your performance?

Results Oriented Grappler

Results Oriented (RO) people are concerned with the outcome. They want another victory in the win column; to be called champion and most importantly they don't want to lose. Their desire to win is so great that the Results Oriented person may adopt a win at any cost approach and not consider who is hurt or damaged in their pursuit of success. Results Oriented people as coaches can sometimes be the 'in your face,' 'no excuses' type.

In the academy many people take the RO approach. The new student who thinks that losing a grappling match makes them less of a person, the guy who always refuses to tap and the person who always wants top position or whose guard is so good that they always want to be on the bottom. What about the person who will hold one grip the entire roll and you end up in a five-minute stalemate?

All of the behaviors listed above are Results Oriented approaches. It is difficult to say if it is the right or the wrong approach because it leads to mixed results. A win at all cost mentality often leads to victory in both practice and in competition. I've tapped many times to grappling partners who have exploded into an arm-bar or a foot-lock technique in practice. I've tapped to choke attacks that lasted well over two minutes in regular grappling sessions. I've even had guys place their toes over my mouth in attempts to get an arm-bar and after escaping I had to look for the camera to see if someone was shooting a fetish video.

In other words, I'm saying that I have tapped to a lot of what I consider slightly out of bounds techniques and approaches. In those situations, I believed that my rolling partners wanted the tap even though it didn't seem like fair play and at the risk of my personal safety. Did I consider them bad people? No, not a single one, but I did consider some of their actions as misplaced in the training environment.

In the competitive arena, Results Oriented grapplers are right at home. A RO approach makes the grappler determined. It makes them work harder when it counts; choose the best strategies for the moment and it makes them a formidable competitor.

Process Oriented Approach

The Process Oriented person, although concerned with success, is also concerned with how that success occurs. They are concerned with their performance during their pursuit and will ask themselves questions such as: Did I perform better than last time or did I improve in the areas I was focusing on? I won, but did I play by the rules and show good sportsmanship? If I keep improving the way I am, will I be a champion?

It is easy to recognize a Process Oriented grappler once you know his/her mindset. It is the person in class who continually works the weak spots in his game, even when he knows he will lose or will be dominated in a grapple. It is the guy who is calm during rolls even when the other person may be 'raging' for a tap. As a coach the Process Oriented grappler is more concerned with his athletes doing their best and improving as opposed to getting the victory.

You can also say that Process Oriented people focus more on the future while Results Oriented people focus more on the now.

Which approach is better?

In reality, both can be successful and of course there are winners of all types. Common sense would dictate that when dealing with people you are close to (i.e., training partners and teammates) you have to use a Process Oriented approach because you have to respect each other's well-being and treat each other how you would like to be treated. Going all out, at all times, and using the Results Oriented approach in your academy can lead to injuries, loss of training partners and being banned.

Yet, Results Oriented approaches can be useful in establishing a pecking order when first grappling with someone or during an in-house competition. It can also give the false appearance that someone is better than he or she is (which can lead to promotions) because they are always tapping people out. But as a general rule, it is my contention that it will leave a grappler with holes in her game as the concern is with winning and not developing an overall game.

However, always using the Process Oriented approach can lead to a person never developing that "win at all cost" mentality that is sometimes necessary in competition and absolutely vital in self-defense situations. It also can lead to people gaining a mental advantage over the Process Oriented grappler because ultimately a tap is a tap. Once people tap you a hierarchy is established whether or not you let them tap you or placed yourself in a position where you would likely be tapped. (I believe that this approach can hinder rank advancement as well.)

So, which is best? It depends on your aims and goals? But how you approach grappling will determine your longevity, your relationships and your overall success.

Ultimately, the approach you take depends on the context and on you.

Now, this is by no means settled. What are your thoughts? What type of grappler are you and how do you think it affects your training and overall success?

The Importance of Winning in the Gym

We all know that Purple or Brown belt in the gym that *can't* beat anyone, but has been practicing so long and tries so hard that they receive sympathy promotions. No one wants to be that guy. I would venture most people would rather be a Blue belt who can tap Purples and Browns rather than a Brown Belt who is always tapped by Whites and Blues.

Why? It is because winning matters.

It matters a lot! I am not saying that one should develop a win at any cost attitude. I am saying that there are a lot of benefits that result as a consequence of winning. In the article, *The Psychology of Winning and Losing* the author describes Psychologist Ian Robertson's description of what happens when a person wins. The following occurs:

Increased testosterone
Increased dopamine levels
Increased well being

You literally become a more capable and happier person. The exact opposite happens to the person who loses.

This may seem like common sense. However, in submission grappling, we often hide our true emotions. It is rare to see a grappler (in class) negatively react to being tapped. As grapplers, we understand that we win some and lose some and it comes with the territory. But deep down, that doesn't make us feel better. It can also make us complacent.

Don't adopt the attitude that this is just training and it doesn't matter if I get the tap out or if I am tapped. It does matter. As you know, winning increases your position in the pecking order; advances you in the quest for a higher belt and provides you with a nice reputation in your gym. However, it also makes you stronger as well as makes you feel better.

Be a good sport, but remember gym wins matter too.

Team Excellence

Team.

Psychologists Tracy Veach and Jerry May describes a team as, "more than merely a group; it's a coordinated ensemble that cooperates to achieve a common goal..."

All people who achieve great things have them, even if they are behind the scenes. Politicians, authors, fighters, CEOs all have individuals, seen and unseen, who provide counseling, training and a host of other support services; including a kick in the pants if necessary.

In life, no one can survive on their own and for great accomplishments we all need people to help us along the way. But beyond the ordinary roles people play in helping one achieve a dream, sometimes we need a group of individuals specifically devoted to our cause. People who know what the mission is; know how to achieve it or have a plan; and are willing to put their time and energies into making it happen.

Do you have your own specific team for grappling? People who have committed to ensuring you reach your grappling goals. Not just a place where you train that has an instructor and people you train with. I am referring to people who you have had a specific conversation and agreement with about being on your team.

A great team can provide wisdom and insight; they can guide you in the right direction; and they can hold you steady when you are not at your best. A great team helps fill in the gaps in knowledge and skills you don't possess and can make sure that you will become well rounded.

As I mentioned before, I am an academic. Anyone who knows me understands that obtaining a doctoral degree was very important to me. However, the process was long (nearly five years) and rigorous. To outsiders and even family and friends it probably seemed as if I was in it by myself because I was always away researching or studying or writing around them. Yet, what they didn't witness was the superb team that led me through my doctoral program. I had a committee of four professors (that I asked to be on my team and who agreed) who pointed out skill sets and a knowledge base I would have to master before moving on to each level. They also provided much needed direction, counsel and tips on how to proceed through the maze that is the dissertation process.

They met with me constantly to monitor my progress and provided the necessary nudges I needed when the time arose. They even pointed me to outside experts who could further help in my journey. Without their high expectations and standards, I would have never have achieved what I have thus far.

Now, as a professor, I also serve as a team member for students.

Question

So as a grappler, who is on your team? -- Is there something that you're attempting solo that could be better achieved with the help of others?

If so, reconsider.

Assemble a network of people who can lead you in the right direction. A group that can support you in becoming the best you can be. Get the best people you can and let them help you lead yourself to success.

The Law of Diminishing Returns and Brazilian Jiu-Jitsu

The Law of Diminishing Returns is an economic concept that asserts that after a certain point, further investment (or effort) does not increase your expected return. In fact, it can reduce it.

I first encountered this term, in relation to grappling, at an academy I was training at in Macon, Georgia. I was training with Rick, better known as Bumble Bee. Bumble Bee was 6'6, 290 pounds and the nicest guy you would want to meet. The thing is, it would be nice to meet him in a regular setting. You don't necessarily want to deal with him in a grappling session.

If I were closer to Bumble Bee's size, then grappling against him would not have been a problem. However, I was six inches shorter than he was and 70 pounds lighter. I was at a serious disadvantage. But at 6 ft., 220 pounds, I was the biggest of the smaller guys so I was always, and I mean always paired with Rick.

When we squared off to roll against each other the same thing happened every time. We would slap hands and end up in a clinch. He would push me onto my back and I would pull guard. He would then dig his elbows into my thighs to make me open my legs. (This simple technique doesn't usually work when going up against a person of similar build, but his size and strength made it feel as if I had two spears digging into my thighs.) After that he would pass into side control. We would then spend the next five to ten minutes with him lying on top of my sternum until he could secure the Kimura. Rinse and repeat.

My instructor Cam, witnessing my struggles week in and out, told me in his southern twang, "Bakari, you're bumping up against the Law of Diminishing Returns." He told me I might be a small guy when compared to Bumble Bee but I was relatively big when compared to the other guys in class. He said that the smaller guys could use their flexibility, speed and small amounts of space to get out of danger when wrestling Rick. However, the closer someone got to Bumble Bee's size and strength they gave up speed, flexibility and the ability to create space.

He told me I was using my assets to my disadvantage. Unfortunately, I was at the point where my strength and size (although good for an average size opponent) was a detriment when facing Bumble Bee. Why? Matching strength was a no-no since his power dwarfed mine. Also, his size nullified any girth tricks I could try to employ. Further, if I were to gain anymore size, it would further inhibit my ability to create space.

In other words, Bumble Bee possessed strength and size in 'spades.' I would be wasting my time trying to match gifts that he naturally and easily produced. My best bet against Bumblebee would be to improve my flexibility, increase my speed, become leaner and refine my technical ability. (This is what BJJ is about anyway.)

Although I learned a lesson from rolling with my nearly 300 pound grappling buddy in Georgia, I still did not fully grasp how the Law of Diminishing Returns could apply to grappling until a year later. By this point I was living in Florida and training at a new academy. It was my first time being able to train with a gi. My previous four year of training (not including Judo) had been no-gi. After eight months my professor let me know that I could test for a belt. I couldn't wait as I was very tired of people looking at my White Belt and assuming that I knew nothing.

I naturally assumed that I would be receiving a Blue Belt, but after testing I was informed that I would be receiving four stripes on my White Belt instead. I was also told that I could re-test again in three months for my Blue Belt.

I wanted that Blue Belt.

A fire lit in me like no other time in my previous four years of grappling. I increased the number of times I went to class each week and I drilled 100 techniques every day at home. I did all of these things no matter how I felt after work, no matter what else needed to be accomplished that day and regardless of how my body felt.

I didn't want any surprises.

Needless to say, by the time of the test, my shoulders were creaking and my neck popped every time I turned my head to the left. I was sore all of the time and walked with a slight limp. I was a complete mess. Yet, I did earn my Blue Belt.

But looking back, I probably would have received the Blue Belt anyway. I believe I was ready for it when I first tested. When I first arrived at the academy I was able to tap all but one of the guys who were testing for Blue Belt my first go around. I also possessed the requisite technical ability and had trained in Judo, which definitely helped my Brazilian Jiu-jitsu. But these guys had been training there for a year or more and I had only been there for eight months, so I believe I had to wait my turn. (Hence, the four stripes.)

In my efforts to insure that I would do well during testing I severely over-trained. I trained for a belt promotion as if I were fighting for a UFC championship. But, all I had to do that day was demonstrate 10 different techniques and then grapple a different person every minute for 10 minutes straight.

I was a classic example of overkill!

Recovery and Realizations

It took several months before my shoulders and neck stopped clicking and my limp went away. In fact, a large part of me being able to heal was due to my knee being injured the following week in class. (I folded my leg inward on a 260-pound guy that was trying to pass my guard. My knee folded in like a toothpick snapping. The pain caused an out of body experience and I emitted a scream that I am still ashamed of to this day. As a result, I had to stop training for five weeks before I could return.)

But that time away from BJJ helped me learn valuable lessons about grappling and more specifically, Brazilian Jiu-jitsu. I realized that I needed to pace myself and to be patient and that the art of grappling is akin to running a marathon and not a sprint. I realized that I can't force people to promote me. There are politics and traditions that no amount of skill or attendance in class will overcome. Further I learned that over-training in attempts to get good (for individual growth) or for advancement and recognition (belt ranking) only leads to burnout, injuries and disappointment when it doesn't happen as expected. As my current Professor always says, "Jiu-jitsu is a Haaaaard sport! It's the hardest sport I have ever been involved with."

Final Thought

We all have different goals with grappling but regardless of our desired outcomes we need to take a balanced approach in our efforts to avoid becoming a victim of The Law of Diminishing Returns.

Stretch Projects

Cal Newport, a best-selling writer and author of the blog, *Study Hacks*, studies ways people can achieve ultimate success. In one of his posts, he mentions a 2003 study of ice skaters detailing what separated top performers from mediocre skaters. The researchers, Cobley and Deakin, found that the top performers worked on the hardest movements (jumps) the majority of practice while the mediocre skaters practiced things they were already good at.

It was the focus on learning difficult tasks that propelled them to the next level. Those who focused on the easy tasks occupied the level of the journeyman in the sport.

Okay, so let's switch to grappling.

When you practice, what do you concentrate on? Do you always seek to tap people with your go to move? Do you use a bodily trait, such as weight, strength or flexibility to the detriment of other skills that could be cultivated? Do you do what comes easy, instead of what's hard? Granted, it is a good idea not to ignore your strengths and to make sure they are polished. However, ignoring your weaknesses can lead to gaping holes in your game that will eventually be exposed, especially if you wish to become an elite player.

To address such deficiencies Newport suggests that you create stretch projects where you focus on working on something you couldn't do previously or can barely do. Additionally, he suggests that you do it within a time frame that's achievable, but challenging. The goal is to always push yourself to be better, but make sure it is achievable.

Many of us rely on our go to moves and techniques that allow us to be big fish in our small ponds. However, doing this will make us similar to the MMA fighters who are one trick ponies who rely solely on their NCAA wrestling talent or championship Muy Thai kickboxing experience. Initially, they have much success and can get away with dominating lesser opponents, but as they face tougher competition they meet guys who can do it all and these one dimensional guys begin to lose. As they fall back down the ladder and time passes, the newer guys become more well-rounded and if the older fighters don't evolve they will lose to the new guys too. It is a cycle that is hard to break and you see it again and again and again.

Don't be that guy! Push yourself to learn more, to grow and to do the difficult things. Life rewards those who challenge themselves.

Poetry as Grappling Therapy

It is poets, not I, who discovered the unconscious. – **Sigmund Freud**

The above quote was provided by Temma Ehrenfeld, in an article posted by *Psychology Today*. Ehrenfeld is a science writer and in her article she discussed the psychological benefits of writing poetry. Poetry can help a person to:

Work through conflict
Express anger or remorse
Record excitement
Declare one's love; and
Entertain others

As an aside, one of the courses I teach as a Professor is Public Speaking. During the semester I have the students write a poem and present it in class. Before they deliver their poem I ask them to talk about their thought process before creating it. Many of them express that they had just had an argument with their roommate or that they were working through a difficult issue or just were feeling silly. Whatever the motivation, they found that creating the poem was cathartic and gave them a sense of fulfillment.

Submission wrestlers are people too. We also have our issues that we have to deal with as grapplers. Some of the problems we deal with are injuries, being unable to train, plateaus, not being promoted and slumps. However, we also have many great things we experience as well.

Poetry is a great tool to express our feelings, work through issues and if nothing else it can be used to entertain others who train in our art. Try it out and if you want, share it with others. I think it will add to everyone's grappling experience.

Using an Audience to Improve in Competition - Brazilian Jiu-jitsu

Picture a man competing in three bicycle races. One is where he rides solo for time. The second is where he uses a "pacer" to help him maintain a consistent speed. In the third race he races against other cyclists. Which of his times will be fastest?

Norman Triplett, believed by many to be the pioneer of sports social psychology, discovered that "competition" affects "performance." Bluntly, you perform at a higher level when other people are present. He discovered that professional cyclists achieved faster times when racing against other riders. Their times became slower when they were timed in solo events or used pacers.

But that's just the tip of the iceberg. Numerous researchers who followed in Triplett's wake received results that supported and debunked his conclusions. Sometimes people performed well when an audience was around, other times they failed miserably. It was Robert Zajonc, Ph.D. (pronounced as Xyience) who came along and found that if you have no talent for a task, your performance level will decrease when an audience is present. On the other hand, it would increase if you were well skilled.

In an oft-cited study (Micheals et al), pool players were classified into two categories; below average and above average. Their games were observed with no audience present and then with four observers milling around. What they found was telling. The above average players scores increased when an audience was present while the below average players scores nose-dived.

So what could this mean for grapplers? Well as beginning grapplers, having guests and friends accompany you to competitions is good for moral support and it demonstrates that they care for you. However, as far as competition is concerned, it may have a deleterious effect on your performance. Having a five-year old screaming, "Get up Daddy!" when pinned in side control as a beginner may short-circuit a grappler's thought process.

But for the intermediate and advanced grappler, as experiments in other fields have indicated, having family and friends present at grappling competitions may be the extra push needed in order to perform better.

Additionally, some people may ask, "What about the people already present at tournaments? Aren't they an audience?" To those individuals I would ask them to reflect on the low attendance rate of 'fans' at grappling events. Participants often outnumber the fans. Further, many matches occur at once. As a consequence, grapplers often end up on mats at the far end of gyms or the other side of an arena where fans will not be present. A grappler could end up with no audience at all.

Therefore, if you do want people present, you should make sure to invite them.

Beat the Competition: Grapple when you Sleep!

During sleep we literally think laterally, untethered by earthly laws **– Gayatri Debi, M.D.**

Let's say there are two grapplers, Devlin and Kris. In the night class their instructor, Dahveed, tells them that a new spot is opening up on the competition team. Who gets it will be based on an in-house competition in two months. The competition will consist of demonstrating techniques and sparring. Devlin and Kris are extremely excited because they have been eyeing a spot on the team for a while now. Plus, the position comes with a stipend and sponsorship. Dahveed provides them with a sheet of new techniques he wants them to learn during the next two months and demonstrate at the competition.

At this moment they are equal in size, strength, and skill and neither Kris nor Devlin has an edge on each other. In the time they have known each other neither has been able to tap the other out. Both want to be champions so they dive with equal fervor into their preparation. Unknowingly, they adopt the same training regimen and practice an equal amount of time. Their diets are virtually the same.

However, this is where their similarities end. Devlin and Kris are two very different people in one key area. That area is rest and sleep. Devlin has always been very disciplined about going to bed early and insuring that he gets 8 hours of sleep. Kris is a night owl and stays up late watching TV and reading books. He usually gets 5 hours of sleep each night.

Who do you think would perform better at the competition?

Although anything could happen in a grappling competition I would root for Devlin. You may wonder, if (from the beginning of preparation) Devlin and Kris are equal in all areas and their training methods, length of training and eating habits are exactly the same, why is it more likely that Devlin would perform better at the competition than Kris?

According to, *Your Brain: The Missing Manual*, Kris is missing out on a precious benefit gained during sleep that would boost his grappling ability. That precious gift is the brain reviewing the previous day's activities and increasing Kris's ability to perform those actions better the next time he tries them.

As we practice any activity neural pathways are created that help the brain to remember how to perform the action at a later date. Each time we perform a particular task the pathways become a stronger series of networks that can help us get the job done. This apparently happens even when we're sleeping.

So by sleeping three more hours would Kris perform just as well as Devlin?

Most likely.

But there's a catch to improving performance by sleeping. The 'review process' occurs during the Rapid Eye Movement (REM) phase of sleep. That is one of four stages of sleep we cycle through throughout the night. It is also the deepest level of sleep. If Kris does not cycle through the REM stages, then he can't reap the benefits.

The author of *Your Brain*,' Matthew MacDonald, cites two studies, one involving rats and the other humans, that demonstrate the effectiveness of REM sleep in improving our ability to conduct tasks we perform during the day. In a study (2001), rats, that had "electrodes implanted" in their brains, were sent through a series of mazes. Their neuronal activity was "recorded." When the rats later fell into REM sleep those same neurons fired in the same way as if they were running the mazes.

Another experiment, conducted by Robert Stickgold (Harvard Medical School) in 2000, had subjects play Tetris (a video game of falling blocks) for 7 hours a day. Participants were observed while sleeping and awakened during their REM cycles. Many of the test subjects were indeed dreaming of playing Tetris (17 of 27). MacDonald goes on to say that in these types of studies, subjects who are prevented from going into REM sleep do not perform as well as others who are allowed REM sleep when learning "new tasks." This provides indications that the REM cycle is needed to gain the benefits of getting more sleep.

The example of Kris and Devlin is a simple mind experiment. And, yes, studies need to be conducted to see how the effect of more REM sleep would affect grapplers when they train. But preliminary evidence already exists that sleep and more specifically, REM sleep, can improve performance.

Sometimes succeeding in something boils down to small advantages. Since grappling is a rough sport and taxing on the body we can only practice for so long or in so many ways. If I can gain an edge through a relaxing, deep sleep, someone please, hand me a pillow.

Smiling and Competition

According to a study conducted by Michael Kraus and David Chen (via BPS Research Digest), MMA fighters who smile at the "pre-fight" matchups are "more likely" to lose their fight.

Coders for the study were asked to assess whether fighters were smiling during their pre-fight matchups (without knowing the fighters or the outcome of the bout). Then the researchers studied UFC statistics and found that the smiling fighters were more likely to lose their fights. The results were not major, but enough to question if the findings have merit.

According to the BPS Research Digest, fighters who bared their teeth were "more likely" to be:

1) "Knocked down"
2) Wrestled to the mat; and
3) Hit more times

The fighters who hadn't smiled were "more likely" to "excel and dominate" according to the BPS Digest article.

The article also stated that people who bet on fights tend to favor the non-smiling fighter as well. The researchers posit that smiling is a cue to the other fighter that you are submissive, lack aggressiveness and lack hostility.

I find this very interesting and wonder if it also applies to BJJ and submission grappling by default. Maybe that smile you give to your opponent as you shake hands is a signal of deference in a competition. What happens if both fighters smile?

This would be a great research project for budding BJJ scholars.

Worse than Average

A common refrain amongst grapplers is, "I suck!" I have heard this constantly throughout my grappling days from Judo, to no-gi to Brazilian Jiu-Jitsu. It's not just new guys who make these claims either. I have witnessed many veteran grapplers adopt this attitude toward their grappling skills. However, I think this approach to assessing one's grappling skills is fraught with misjudgments.

Psychologist Jeremy Dean, in his article entitled, *The Worse than Average Effect: When you are better than you think*, discusses this theory of the same name. Dean discusses the tendency of people to downgrade their abilities, compared to others, when it comes to stereotypically hard tasks (e.g., submission wrestling). The examples he provides are computer programming, telling a funny story or playing chess. However, most people tend to overestimate their abilities when it comes to stereotypically easy things such as bicycle riding and driving a car.

The logic is easy to follow when you ponder it for a bit. An overwhelming majority of adults who can drive, do. Additionally, bike riding is a pretty universal activity as well. Many bike riders as well as drivers think that they are better drivers than the rest of us. Yet, with so many people doing the same thing, how would you know?

However, when it comes to grappling, how many people in the world can really say that they have picked up another human being and then slammed them on the ground? Outside of your grappling circle, how many of your family members and friends have held people down hundreds or thousands of times. What non-grappler do you know has escaped people hundreds of times (or even once) trying to bend one of his limbs just to the point of it snapping? Even if you are a new grappler and have only done these things a few dozen times, you most likely have more experience than the average human being on earth.

Grapplers are humble, the sport quickly teaches us to be. It is very difficult to believe you are invincible when at some point in every practice you are being submitted, manhandled or thoroughly controlled. However, viewing ourselves from this small window can be misleading if we don't recognize the skill we are building and how we are really in an exclusive club as grapplers. Most people can't do what you do. They haven't put the time in.

You don't have to be cocky, but you should be confident in your abilities and skills. Remember the gym is a place to learn. At times it will be difficult to learn, but that is what makes it so easy when you compete or are forced to use your skills elsewhere.

Rationalization

Andre Agassi in his book, *Open*, described a ritual he performed before every tennis match in order to prepare for 'battle.' He would take a shower and tell himself how great he was, how he could do anything and that he was unbeatable. --- Agassi admitted that he was psyching himself out and that he was filling himself with "hot water courage." He also opined that he would have never been able to achieve the amazing feats that define his career without these talks.

What Agassi was doing is known as intrapersonal communication. The internal conversations we have with ourselves about nearly everything. Only he was doing it in a way to increase his productivity.

As grapplers, it is easy to allow a bad day or minor setbacks to cloud our judgment or lead us to doubt our abilities. It is common sense that if you think negatively then you will feel negatively about yourself or something you have to do. But common sense is one thing and what you actually do is another. It is very easy to get trapped into patterns of thinking that are self-defeating and in some cases debilitating to your ability to perform on the mat.

This is where Cognitive Restructuring may be of help. Cognitive Restructuring is the process of identifying irrational and crippling thought processes and replacing them with thoughts that properly reflect the situations a person is dealing with. This method helps a person to manage the emotions they are experiencing and to make decisions that increases their quality of life.

Albert Ellis, Ph.D. and Derek Harper, Ph.D., who are considered pioneers in the field of Rational Emotive Therapy (Cognitive Restructuring), claimed there are three ways to affect your emotions. One is through the use of drugs and chemicals to alter your mood. The second way is through physical exercise as it regulates hormones that help the body to manage stress and the brain releases chemicals that give the person exercising a high. The third is monitoring one's thoughts and making sure they are in sync with ideas that will keep you alive and enjoying the life that you are living. Submission grapplers already use one of the three as we are in a physically demanding sport. It is the third way, monitoring thoughts, which we should also include in our training.

Professionals who use Rational Emotive Therapy do not discount the use of physical exercise and prescribed drugs as an effective means to manage emotional states, especially for serious mental disorders. But as the pioneers Ellis and Harper claimed, drugs and exercise are not looked upon as permanent solutions to dealing with feelings and emotions that a person may feel overwhelmed by. A comparable parable would be, "Give a man a fish and he eats for one day. Teach him how to fish and he can eat for a lifetime." In this instance, teaching a man to fish is teaching him how to restructure his thoughts in order to stay sane and see things rationally.

I used cognitive restructuring all the time in my training because I know that looking at a problem at face value doesn't always give me the proper perspective. For instance, I once came to practice and received a beating from just about everyone who was there. I struggled against everyone. To make it worse, there were a couple of guys who I hadn't seen in a few months and they manhandled me. I was disgusted with myself on the drive home because everything was off. My muscles gave out, my cardio was non-existent and I had to resort to stalling just to make it through sparring.

Fortunately, I quickly realized that I was slipping into negativity so I calmed down. I then began to think of reasons why I had a bad day. I had been working out by lifting weights and playing sports all year so that wasn't the reason. I had been coming regularly to class so I hadn't fallen behind in skill level. The other guys who I hadn't seen in a while had not been training and they didn't surprise me with anything new. Then it hit me! I had been sick the week before where I had headaches, chills, fever and a cold. I had been down all week. Even though it was Friday of the following week, I realized that I hadn't fully recovered.

I immediately felt better and realized that I hadn't fully bounced back yet, hence I had my behind handed to me in class. Taking the time to rationally think through my problem allowed me to re-evaluate my situation and not become despondent about what happened.

Cognitive Restructuring is a great tool to use with sport related issues. As mentioned before, Andre Agassi used it to build himself up, reminding himself of all of the times he had overcome odds and had succeeded at higher than average levels. We can also use Cognitive Restructuring to realistically view our problems and to make reasoned decisions when addressing them.

Change the Story (Rank and Advancement)

I am a huge Seth Godin fan, who is an expert on marketing and advertising, and recently he penned a blog post titled, *The Facts*. He wrote:

"The story wins the day every time… Your position on just about everything, including…your salary, your stock options, your credit card debt and your mortgage are almost certainly based on the story you tell yourself, not some universal fact from the universal fact database. ---Not just you, everybody."

Godin is referring to the idea that how you craft the narrative determines your outcome. Further, he asserts that it affects every aspect of your life.

So what's your grappling story? If your friends were gathered around the campfire and you had to tell a tale about your grappling life, what would you say? More importantly, what are you telling yourself?

All day we are in unceasing conversations with ourselves. Further, as submission wrestlers, we tell ourselves who we are, how good we are, what we should do, how we should respond and what our mission is. This intrapersonal communication governs our grappling experiences to a huge extent and affects our overall well-being. When things are good and especially when they are great the internal dialogue is most likely positive and helps move us forward. But what about when things aren't going according to plan?

It is in these times that we need to re-evaluate our internal conversations and monitor what we are saying to see what it really going on.

Role Theory asserts that there are a multitude of 'characters' that exist in our world. Some of these roles we are born into (e.g., family relationships) and others we willingly accept (marriage, jobs, friendships). Others are foisted upon us, such as stereotypes, or we are pressured into, such as competing with neighbors. In Brazilian Jiu-Jitsu, Sambo, Judo and other grappling arts, we are issued belt rankings and other rules that prescribe behavior and how we are to interact with others. Grappling social norms often dictate that we accept these roles and conform to certain standards of behavior that define them.

This is great when you're 'Winning!' However, what do you do when your thought process and your roles are crushing your well-being? As a White belt do you sabotage your efforts because not much is expected of you? As a Blue belt do you lose to Purple belts because you unconsciously defer? As a Purple belt, do you hold back on tapping out a higher-ranking grappler or your instructor because of the respect factor?

In grappling, there are so many ways we can let our assigned roles hinder our progress. If you are having this issue, examine what you are telling yourself. What you have accepted, are accepting and will accept in the future is based on who you think you are. To change that, you have to consciously alter the story of *whom you think you are* to fit the concept of *who you want to be*. Then act accordingly!

Now, this is not always easy because our habits and behaviors have crept upon us. We often miss the shifts as they occur. For instance, after high school or college we may stop playing sports or become less active and stop thinking of ourselves as athletes. When we get into a relationship many of us stop doing the things that we did to stay attractive in the eyes of potential mates when we were single. We no longer strive to be or consider it necessary to be 'sexy.' Similarly, at a certain point in our grappling lives we may begin to think things such as, "I don't need to worry about tapping him out, he's a Purple Belt." Or "She's a Black Belt, I don't have a chance." Slowly, we begin to think how we believe a person in our 'role' (White belt, Blue belt, etc.) is supposed to think and we act accordingly.

Yet, once you start telling yourself a different story then those ideas begin to change. By adopting a new role or a different way of looking at a current one you can exact new standards that can improve your quality of life. For instance, you can start looking at yourself as that Blue Belt that can tap out any Purple Belt. Or you can say to yourself that "The 'belt' is just a mirage, I can tap anything that walks on two legs, maybe four!" Whether you can do it or not at this point is immaterial. You have to change the image you hold of yourself and then adjust to that new reality you have prescribed.

Besides, it is easier to alter our stories than it is to resort to exhausting tactics such as willpower for change. Willpower is fleeting, subject to mood and how much discipline you can exert. Your story and the role you assign yourself is something that will influence you as long as you maintain it.

If your current circumstances aren't to your liking, change your story and your circumstances will change too.

Role Theory, Grappling and Age

At a certain age many of us buy into the idea that it is too late or that we are too old to do something different than what we have always done. We will deny ourselves the opportunity to try a new job or career; a new hobby, a sport or a relationship because we think too much time has passed us by. For grapplers, this can happen at any age 20, 30, 40, etc.

Or we accept the crippling idea that we are too old to continue doing what we love to do. We let our age; social norms and other people's perception of what our role in life should be govern our decisions even if there is ample evidence to the contrary. I think Herschel Walker's story can show us why we need to re-evaluate these types of thoughts and use a more balanced approach when evaluating our age and what we think we can do and accomplish.

At 48 years old, Herschel Walker defeated Scott Carson in a professional Mixed Martial Arts bout. It was Walker's second fight and second victory. It is not amazing that Herschel Walker won the fight. Nor is it special that he was 48. It is not even noteworthy that he was competing in an extremely hard sport for a top organization, because many people get the chance.

Yet, when you put all of those variables together Herschel Walker becomes a very interesting man. Walker is a former college football standout that played for the University of Georgia and won the Heisman Trophy. He then played 15 years of professional football in the NFL and the now defunct USFL. He also competed in the 1992 Olympics as a bobsledder for the United States where he and his teammate placed 7th. But those achievements occurred in his teens, twenties and thirties.

Now, over a decade later he has entered a new sport, which is considered a young man's game and has started over again. Herschel Walker calls himself a "rookie" and admits that he is very "young" to Mixed Martial Arts. He also knew he had the potential to embarrass himself by becoming a mixed martial artist. As a public figure he was also aware that many in the media would treat his entry into the world of fighting as a spectacle and coverage could be less than flattering. In an AOL article, reporter Ben Fowlkes provides a quote from Herschel Walker:

"I knew this was really hard. I think there are so many people taking this as a joke. But I knew, all the athletes who think they could just step into this, that's crazy. These guys are serious. They put the time in, and you've got to respect that. When I came into the gym, I was a rookie again. I didn't have a black belt in Taekwondo. I didn't have a Heisman Trophy. I had to mop the floors and earn my stripes all over again."

Walker was right. In fact, before his first fight, his foray into the sport had been labeled as a "freak show." But Herschel Walker took the plunge and endured the changes he needed to make in order to become a professional Mixed Martial Artist.How many of us would take a chance like that?

In the previous section, I briefly discussed Role Theory, now I want to use Walker's story as an opportunity to give it a more formal definition. We all 'play' roles in life similar to characters in a play. These roles (or should I say rules) govern our behavior and determine how we will interact with family members, in our personal relationships and in our dealings at work, school and society at large. These roles are often accepted willingly because they help maintain peace and stability and from a moral standpoint would be considered the proper thing to do, such as parents providing care for their children or a spouse protecting one's mate. However, sometimes we don't accept roles for an altruistic purpose. Instead we accept them because "that's just the way it is."

As a result, many of us forget all of the positive modes of thinking that allowed us to become successful and gradually adopt the mindset required of the roles we accept. Then we stop taking the actions that make our current life possible or could make our desired new life a reality. Before you know it we fit our roles exactly.

But it doesn't have to be that way. People like Herschel Walker or Olympic swimmer, Dara Torres, who won Olympic medals at age 41 have demonstrated what is possible. Or if those two aren't convincing enough what about Ken Minks, the 73 year old, who tried out and made the basketball team at Roane State Community College?

The message is not that we all have the capability to become star athletes regardless of age. It is that, as grapplers we have goals, dreams and unfulfilled wishes that we sometimes give up on because we accepted someone's notion of who we should be and what we can accomplish. Don't let age define you or cause you to behave differently 'just because." We have to be realistic, but we also have to do self-evaluations and not let others determine what we should and should be doing.

Positive Contributions

Each of us has a meter inside, where we consciously or unconsciously measure the balance of give and take that exists in our relationships. When dealing with our coaches, teammates and training partners we all gauge the level of positive reciprocity that exists. Further, if we are conscientious we must also remember that how we behave when doing something for someone is also important.

The term, interactional justice, is used by organizational psychologists to describe how willing an organization or person is to perform an act for another and how the receiver feels he or she was treated during the exchange. As the person who gives, we often concentrate on the "benefits" that the other person will receive.

However, as a receiver we place greater value on how a service is provided. If the provider performed the act begrudgingly then as a receiver we feel less of an obligation to return the favor (Baron, Byrne & Branscombe, 2006).

As a coach, instructor or senior student do you give willingly when a lower ranked student asks a question or do you blow the person off or act like it is a bother to address her question? They notice. As a student, do you help out by being conscientious and pay close attention during drills, attend class regularly and give respect to not only your instructors, but also your fellow classmates? I ask this because everyone is paying attention as givers and receivers.

To judge the balance of give and take in a relationship and how willing a person is to do something for us is not selfishness. It can be, but in healthy relationships it is natural to want to do our fair share and to be treated fairly; especially if we truly appreciate and value the other person or institution.

If we value others we make sure that we are a team player and show up on time and add value to collaborative projects (training for competitions or preparing for promotions). We also make sure that training partners or higher-ups are not left 'holding the bag' or have to clean up our mistakes. In our interactions in the gym we make sure we are friendly and outside the gym we ensure that we show up for parties or special events and alternate who picks up the tab for lunch or dinner if the occasions arise. We also check up on training buddies when we haven't seen them for a while.

As a grappler, if you are conscientious of your need to maintain the give and take balance in relationships, congratulations! However, from time to time, we need to review all of our behavior to see if we are providing positive contributions or if we are taking more than we are giving.

If we are accepting more than we give, then we must re-balance that relationship. Sometimes we aren't mindful of a senior student that we always allow to handle certain difficult tasks because they "do it so well." Or a mentor who always provides advice and instruction but only receives a big, "Thanks man!" in return.

Seeking a give and take balance is the best way to keep relationships thriving, healthy and to ensure growth for everyone involved. -- Have you contributed, positively, to your grappling relationships lately?

Your Influence as a Grappler

Nexus, *Connected*, *Outliers*, *Linked*, *The Social Atom* and *Six Degrees* are all books that discuss how social ties and networks affect us in ways that we can't begin to imagine. Additionally, each new study similar to Stanley Milgram's "Small World" (six degrees of separation) experiment keeps academics and laypersons mesmerized at how closely we are all interconnected.

A lot of research in this field deals with how we can benefit from understanding the underlying frameworks of networks, whether it is a work organization, an institution, a social relationship, epidemiology or modes of traffic. Many of the books mentioned above were written by academics, yet at the same time they were created with popular audiences in mind. This approach, I argue, influences authors to suggest how their ideas will help improve lives. Thus, a self-help connection is present in not only books of this type but also in the interpretation by a large portion of those who buy them.

Further, it has been my experience that most of the ideas discussed around social ties and networks are issued with the intent of demonstrating how networks can be beneficial from the **outside-in**. For example: How to position yourself to get noticed by upper management; Associates or acquaintances can help you find a job quicker than family and friends; 'It's not what you know, but whom you know.' Or the advice concerning social ties may be used to convince you to stay out of trouble such as; you can avoid many hassles by choosing the proper friends or if your friend's friend gains weight then you will too. Or in some cases, you may find that you will gain benefits due to your associations.

What I often find missing in a lot of discussions concerning social networks is a focus on **how the individual can affect his network for positive change**. In other words, many of us often ask how can we position ourselves so we can benefit the most and not **how others can benefit by being acquainted with us**.

Relate this to grappling for a moment, when is the last time you assessed all of the benefits that people get from knowing you? Further, if you have, do you keep a list handy to remind you of those benefits? It is easy, at first glance, to think that this can quickly become an egotistical exercise, but that depends upon the intention. I argue the opposite of that assumption and assert that assessing the benefits one offers to his or her gym, competition team and training mates in general is a great way to learn one's strengths and weaknesses. It is also a more balanced approach in the pursuit to obtain success than to always be jockeying for position and rank without little thought to what value you can add for others.

Regardless of one's position or station in the grappling organization, thinking about the ways that you are of benefit to others is a great exercise to keep you moving forward. It will not only help you improve the games of your training buddies, but also your own.

Hook Value: Coaches and Future Owners

Think about your friends and associates. Each one probably has a very useful function. One person may make any situation more fun or tell lots of jokes. Another may keep 'juicy' secrets you have to get off your chest. Someone else may always be willing to play a game of tennis, a few holes of golf or run a trail with you. Another may always be in the know about what's happening in your locale.

But on a slightly more serious note, why are people attracted to you? More specifically, why are people attracted to you as an instructor or coach? What makes people want to work or conduct business with you? Why would people want to become a part of your inner circle or you to become a part of theirs? What makes you memorable and makes people excited to see you? Why would someone want to have the "insert your name" experience again?

In other words, what is your hook and how do you use your hook(s) to improve your business and coaching relationships?

The answer to becoming an attraction is rather simple. To attract, gain access or to be invited again into the business or social circles you are interested in, you have to discover and develop the character traits or qualities that other members will consider valuable. It may seem calculating, but as a business owner or trainer the stakes require it. By understanding this concept and increasing your 'hook value' you can increase your current worth to people you already train and to those who are deciding if they want to train with you.

Your value can be applied in numerous ways. It could be:

Specific Knowledge - Humor - Loyalty - Clutch Performer - Creative Input - Overall Intelligence - Charm - Conversational Ability - Inside Information (legal) - Athletic Ability - Leadership Skills - Networking Ability - Public Speaking Ability - Writing Skills - Marketing Skills - Organizational Skills - Charitable Mindset

Any of these characteristics could be your 'hook.' They can be natural talents that you further develop or non-talents that you cultivate. Either way, if used sincerely and when it counts, your hook should bring more value to other grapplers and your own life, both in business and personally.

Use your 'hook' to your advantage.

Coaches

It can be argued that the most important person in the grappling experience is the coach, whether he goes by the title of Professor, Instructor, Master or Paul. The coach is usually the first person to greet you when you visit a prospective gym, the person to give you the gym's sales pitch and will serve as the ultimate guide in your grappling journey. Coaches matter! The following two sections discuss two issues that are very important to coaching: trust and inspiring confidence.

QUEST: The Coach

The British Psychological Society took a look at research concerning executive coaching and its rate of effectiveness in making people better managers, supervisors, colleagues and employees. Although executive coaching deals with employment, I still feel the study is useful to grapplers as it explored interpersonal relationships, leadership and what people expect when they ask someone to serve as their coach. In Brazilian Jiu-jitsu or grappling in general, we surrender our authority to another person and believe that the person will be able to help us achieve our goals, just as in executing coaching.

What the researchers found is that there is very little evidence to suggest that executive coaching works very well. Part of the reason they say this problem exists is because many people do not write out or solidify what they want to achieve as an individual or with their coach. They just meet and work on different scenarios. (Sound familiar?) Yes, the executive coach does have an idea of what is needed, but the client is who is being served.

The same finding could be applied to grappling. How many of us have coaches that have asked us what did we want to achieve by training in grappling? If the question was asked, did it go beyond a short conversation? Was a session devoted to what you wanted or was anything written down? Most likely, students are placed into a generic training format that is formed arbitrarily.

Even though very little evidence was found to substantiate that executive coaching works and much of the executive coaches' claims were not based on evidence, researches did find out what clients expected from their coaches. I created the acronym QUEST to sum it up.

QU – Quality relationship
ES– Emotional support
T – Trust

More than anything else, these three factors governed how clients felt about their coaching experiences. This mattered more than the content provided. That may sound counterintuitive, but ponder it for a second.

Unless most grappling bloggers are just playing lip service, the common spiel about training is 'BJJ is a marathon, not a sprint' and it is the **journey** that matters. Plus, if you stick with grappling long enough, you know you will be able to reasonably be able to defend yourself. So unless you want to become a world champion or go into MMA, if an instructor is competent, not too much emphasis is placed on style of instruction. Besides, you can learn many things on your own.

However, if you do not have a good **(quality)** relationship with your instructor or the people in your academy, you can develop a sour view toward grappling. Quality deals with your instructor's approachability, friendliness, caring nature and ability to create a mutually beneficial relationship. Quality = Good relations you're your instructor. I once belonged to an academy where the instructor and some of my classmates were decidedly unfriendly. Many didn't say hello when spoken to and would ignore me when I would say goodbye on my way out. After every practice I would leave feeling unsatisfied and my natural endorphin high would be crushed through my interactions with them. I trained with them for six months before going on my way.

Good relations are further buoyed by the **emotional support** your coach provides. An instructor doesn't have to be a 'softee,' as grappling is a combat sport. However, an instructor should help build you up, acknowledge you when you work hard and promote you when you progress to certain levels. Luckily, most of my coaches have been emotionally supportive and have been good coaches. However, this is not the case with everyone.

Finally, **trust** is a vital part of the coach-client relationship. People are surrendering their authority when they enter an academy and allow another grown person to order them around and 'yell' at them to help them reach a goal. Coaches have to be sure that they do not break that trust by misjudging their authority and allowing their tempers to flare, overstepping personal boundaries and violating the mission of helping someone for the sake of business goals. People do not join grappling gyms to make coaches rich, run classes for them and they are not just another number.

In my experience, I have gotten jittery around coaches who seem to forget that we are paying to take classes and are not children. When I see a coach arbitrarily lose his cool toward someone, I get uncomfortable. If they will act like that toward someone else, what makes me any different?

In one place I trained, I had the owner's assistant ask me in front of a crowd if I had paid my dues. I was outraged. Not only had I paid my dues three months in advance the previous week, I had also never been late or missed a payment. In another academy, after I said I did not want to attend a seminar, I was asked why and if it was due to finances. --- As a grown man, I do not have to explain why and the finance question made my stomach turn. I felt it was a sales pressure technique in bad taste. Even though I enjoyed training there, liked the people and the instructor, it was the beginning of the end. I felt that my trust was being violated and the client-coach relationship did not feel safe anymore.

I was progressing at a pretty good clip and learning a lot, so I wrestled with my decision, but ultimately, I chose me over mistreatment. When one of the QUEST factors was violated (or missing) I found myself seeking another home. I wonder if many of you have or would do the same?

Building Confidence: Coaching

In the grappling world we seek the help of others when trying to improve. We take private lessons, find mentors in class, talk to senior students, purchase books, read blogs and watch videos. If we apply the lessons learned through these interactions, there is a big chance we will see improvements.

But what do we do when faced with the task of building up others? At some point in our grappling careers, people begin to look to us for instruction, whether we want them to or not and regardless of our readiness. After accepting this responsibility, we are no longer the coached, a mentee, the counseled or the ronin seeking knowledge. At this stage, others look toward us for growth. How do we help them?

In the book, *Finding Your Zone*, by Michael Lardon, M.D., he discusses psychologist Albert Bandura's process for developing confidence. The steps are:

1. Mastery Experiences
2. Vicarious Learning
3. Modeling Behavior; and
4. Social Persuasion

As a communications professor I use these techniques all of the time. Therefore, I will explain how each works by applying it to one of the courses I teach, Public Speaking.

Mastery Experiences

One of the components necessary to build confidence is previous success in the endeavor you are trying to be successful in. Since my course's ultimate goal is to have students competently deliver three speeches, classes are geared toward providing them with public speaking experience. Each class, students work through short exercises in order to demonstrate that they can speak in front of others and nothing dreadful will occur. Whether it's discussing a current event, telling us about a hobby or interest, or delivering a Public Service Announcement as a group they develop a portfolio of experiences that lets them know that they have succeeded in speaking in front of others before.

When teaching grappling, students should be taught techniques that they can master. The technique should be something that they can use successfully in sparring and something that they can build upon.

Vicarious Learning

This is simply the process of learning through the experiences of others. In training others, a more simple way of explaining vicarious learning would be, "Well if he or she can do it, then I know I can!" In a grappling class this is often accomplished through demonstrating technique. Most of the time, instructors will use the most senior student or their favorite as the uke (one being acted against). However, to shake things up, teach a less advanced student how to do the technique. ("So easy, a caveman can do it.")

Modeling Behavior

This third phase is achieved by finding examples of people who are involved in the same activity, but performing at an extremely high level. By observing the behavior of the highly skilled, the observer 'raises the bar' and sees the potential available to her. In my speech course this is accomplished by analyzing videos of famous public figures and also videos of former students who delivered amazing speeches in previous classes. By critiquing those speeches, we further identify the specific behaviors that the students should mimic.

One coaching technique grappling instructors should consider is analyzing film with students. Fifteen minutes of a class could be devoted to breaking down technique with a question and answer period. Often when instructors coach a technique they are demonstrating it and can't see gaps in their instruction. However, if they show a video that is demonstrating proper technique they can provide pointers that they would miss showing the technique themselves.

Get into the minutiae of the movements and scale it down to its smallest elements. Not only is this a different approach, it also allows the students to get a better grasp of what the technique is before being sent to practice without a clue of how to perform the technique.

Social Persuasion

Lardon describes this as 'positive verbal reinforcement.' We all need encouragement and in many instances a positive word is all someone needs in order to keep going. In my course, I can't say 'good job' every time someone speaks in front of the class and a lot of times it wasn't a 'good job.' Those you have to train will not always perform admirably as well. But what I do at the end of the classroom exercises is thank everyone for their participation and provide positive group assessment.

Consider providing a brief assessment of that day's performance at the end of every grappling session. If someone performed well that day, give her credit. Also, let students know you were paying attention by citing some areas you want to work on (overall) for improvement.

As an aside, in most of my classes, students clap after each person finishes an exercise. I do not suggest or prompt them to do so. The students quickly realize that they are all in the same predicament so they might as well be supportive. I know that clapping is not verbal persuasion but it still makes the person feel that they are in a positive and supportive environment. Encouraging a positive ending after a grappling session is also a good way to build morale and promote goodwill. An example is a class that shakes hands afterwards or performs a ritual where everyone places their hands in the center and shouts something such as "1, 2, 3, HARD WORK, STRONG MIND!"

Final Thoughts

I used my speech course as an example because teaching people how to communicate through speech, media writing, etc., is my specialty. However, the techniques that Lardon shared through Bandura can be applied to grappling settings as well.

Thanks!

I am glad you bought this book and read it to the end. I hope you enjoyed it! Please do me a favor and write a review (Amazon, iTunes and B&N) and let me know how you feel.

Regards,

Bakari Akil II, PhD (aka JiuJitsu365)

Printed in Great Britain
by Amazon

82710789R00062